The Association of the United States Army, a non-profit professional educational association, has worked to support all aspects of national security. AUSA also advances the interests of our men and women who serve and the family members who stand at their side.

Membership is open to all components of the Army: Active, National Guard, Army Reserve, Army Retirees, Government Civilians, ROTC, family members and concerned citizens.

Association of the United States Army
2425 Wilson Boulevard
Arlington, VA 22201
703-841-4300
800-336-4570

UNITED STATES ARMY — AT — WAR

9/11 Through Iraq

F. Clifton Berry, Jr.

Featuring the photography of Dennis Steele, ARMY Magazine photojournalist

Presented by the Association of the United States Army

Naval Institute Press
Annapolis, Maryland

Design by Hinge, Inc., www.studiohinge.com

Naval Institute Press
291 Wood Road
Annapolis, Maryland 21402
www.usni.org

Library of Congress Cataloging-in-Publication Data

Berry, F. Clifton.
  United States Army at war : 9/11 through Iraq / F. Clifton Berry.
     p. cm.
Includes bibliographical references (p.   ) and index.
  ISBN 1-59114-063-3
  1. Iraq War, 2003--Pictorial works. 2. September 11 Terrorist
Attacks, 2001--Pictorial works. 3. War on Terrorism, 2001---Pictorial
works. 4. United States. Army--History--21st century--Pictorial works.
I. Title.
  DS79.762.B47 2003
  973.931--dc22
                                  2003015116

Printed in the United States of America.

10 9 8 7 6 5 4 3 2 1

To all the members of the total
United States Army of the early 21st century, and
to their families. Their selfless service is a magnificent
example for all Americans.

Contents

Foreword

During the past two years we have witnessed a transformation in the world security environment that presents many new challenges to our nation's armed forces. This transformation requires our services to fully integrate across the spectrum of joint operations as we engage in multiple theaters in the global war on terrorism as well as other potential conflicts. Our forces must operate alongside our allies, across a wide range of military capabilities, and varying international political and military command and control structures.

Since 1775, the United States Army has risen to every challenge from Lexington, through regional and world wars, and, more recently, to the mountains of Afghanistan and the streets of Baghdad. The men and women who have served America and the cause of freedom since our homeland was attacked on Sept. 11, 2001, like their forebears have answered their country's call with honor, professionalism, selflessness and valor. These men and women have shown courageous initiative and resolve in the ongoing evolution of global affairs. I am honored to serve with them. I echo their thanks for the support of their families and the many other citizens of our great nation who have stood with us.

The Army has played, and continues to play, a vital role in America's global operations—to include Operation Enduring Freedom and Operation Iraqi Freedom. This role firmly marks transformation—a transformation of equipment, doctrine, training, organization and integration across the battle-space. Today's operations are truly joint. They involve mutual reliance among service components; joint and combined command of ground forces; information operations "netted and nested" from the strategic to the tactical levels of war; integrated simultaneous and serial combat actions; precision effects enhanced by new technologies; and planning flexibility that preempts the enemy's decision cycle.

Afghanistan and Iraq are just the latest stops on the road to the Army's future. On these two very different battlefields, the Army has taken transformational steps, achieving along with our sister services, our nation's military goals rapidly and effectively. However, much work remains to be done in the international security cooperation environment and within our own armed services to guarantee meeting America's national security demands in the remainder of the 21st century. This work will require the best from the Army as we identify and pursue, through a fully joint lens, the qualities of the Army of the future. There is no doubt that we are up to the task.

Tommy R. Franks
General, U.S. Army
Commander, United States Central Command,
July 2000–July 2003

Preface

The United States Army of the 21st century inherited a legacy of service to the nation extending 228 years from the American Revolution. From Lexington to the present, active duty soldiers and minutemen of the reserve components have proven equal to the missions demanded of them. They have protected the United States and advanced the cause of freedom around the world.

The Association of the United States Army created this illustrated book to give the nation a glimpse of the total Army in action. In mid-2003, the Army had more than 235,000 men and women deployed overseas on 200 missions in 50 countries.

One book cannot cover all those missions. Therefore, this book focuses on Army activities in three regions. The first section covers the attack on, and defense of, the homeland from Sept. 11, 2001, onward. Operation Enduring Freedom, the coalition campaign in Afghanistan, comprises the second section. The third part of the book covers Operation Iraqi Freedom from the buildup in Kuwait to combat and its aftermath. Coverage in all sections runs through mid-2003.

Photojournalist Dennis Steele of AUSA's *ARMY Magazine* has for many years created countless articles graced with his photos. Steele visited, lived with and campaigned with the United States Army long before the phrase "embedded journalist" joined the lexicon. He accompanied units in the field and in combat to get the facts and the photos. Many of his images form the foundation of this book.

The majority of images come from photographers of the United States Army and other services, as well as coalition allies. Like Steele, those photographers accompanied the combat forces and supporting units that create mission success.

This book presents only a small selection of the photography covering the United States Army of today. The images shown here have been cleared for public release. Although they depict a wide range of Army activities, these photos are representative, not exhaustive. They are snapshots that give a hint of the activities shown. However impressive visually, they cannot convey the feeling of penetrating cold in the high mountains, or the grit of sand in the nostrils and mouth in the noonday desert, or the intensity of combat.

We hope these pictures and the accompanying information convey a sense of the Army's people and stimulate readers' interest in learning more about them.

F. Clifton Berry, Jr.

Assault and Response

When terrorists attacked the United States with four hijacked commercial airliners on the morning of Sept. 11, 2001, most Americans listened or watched in horror. The United States Army, itself wounded by the attacks, did more than watch and listen. Elements of the total Army—active duty soldiers, National Guard, Army Reserve, civilian employees, families—responded and took action immediately.

Within an hour's time, four attacks struck at the American homeland. Two airliners smashed into the twin towers of New York's World Trade Center and another struck the Pentagon. A fourth hijacked airliner crashed in western Pennsylvania after passengers fought back against the terrorists who seized it.

Citizen soldiers in New York City and nationwide acted. Lt. Gen. H. Steven Blum, chief of the National Guard Bureau in 2003, said, "The National Guard did not wait for a formal call to duty on Sept. 11. Guardsmen all around the nation grabbed their gear and answered the call to the colors. That's what the minuteman tradition is all about."

Active duty soldiers from Fort Hamilton pitched in at Ground Zero, as did Army Reservists. Soon Gov. George Pataki authorized mobilization of the entire New York National Guard for active duty within the state.

In Virginia, all 64 people in the airliner and 125 persons inside the Pentagon died in that attack. Units from the Military District of Washington, including medical, engineer and ordnance personnel, responded. Soldiers from the 3d Infantry Regiment (The Old Guard) from neighboring Fort Myer went on a war footing with civilian responders.

Global terrorism had struck the American homeland. Uncommon courage became commonplace at all disaster sites. The attacks roused Americans nationwide to shared senses of vulnerability and resolve to fight back against terrorism.

As the origins of the Sept. 11 attacks became clear, the Army and its sister services responded to the nation's call. Defense of the homeland against further attacks became a top priority, concurrent with missions to find and destroy the terrorist enemies responsible for the attacks.

◀

Rescue and recovery efforts began immediately after the hijacked 757 airliner smashed into the E-ring of the Pentagon on Sept. 11, 2001.

(Photo by Scott Boatright)

The five floors on the southwest-facing E-ring of the Pentagon sag on Sept. 12, 2001. *(DoD photo by R. D. Ward)*

▲

Secretary of Defense Donald H. Rumsfeld, right, returns to his Pentagon office Tuesday, Sept. 11, 2001, after surveying damage from the hijacked American Airlines Flight 77 that crashed into the building. *(U.S. Army photo by Sgt. Carmen L. Burgess)*

◄

The Pentagon smolders after the terrorist attack. *(Dennis Steele, ARMY Magazine)*

▲

"We're grieving with America," reads the sign as German citizens show solidarity with U.S. troops at Campbell Barracks in Heidelberg, Germany, following the terrorist attacks on Sept. 11, 2001. *(U.S. Army photo)*

▲

Sgt. Maj. David Lamouret of the 204th Combat Engineer Battalion, New York National Guard, instructs one of his soldiers at a security check-point in Lower Manhattan, where the World Trade Center towers collapsed after the Sept. 11 terrorist attacks. Said one firefighter of the guardsmen: "They make our difficult mission a lot easier, and we are proud they're here." *(U.S. Army photo by Paul Morando)*

President George W. Bush thanks the recovery teams at the Pentagon. He and Secretary of Defense Donald H. Rumsfeld, left, stand in front of rescue equipment from Fairfax County, Va.

(Photo by Scott Boatright)

◄ Pentagon, Sept. 17, 2001. Artificial lights illuminate the scene as round-the-clock recovery efforts continue. *(U.S. Army photo by Staff Sgt. John Valceanu)*

◄ Lt. Col. John Flanagan of the New York Army National Guard is a Long Island police detective. Following 9/11, he works in the guard's joint liaison office with New York City's Office of Emergency Management on Pier 92, Manhattan. Flanagan is a veteran of the Navy's submarine service. *(Pete Murphy, AUSA News)*

◄ Firefighters and military personnel unfurl a large American flag from the roof of the Pentagon during the Sept. 12, 2001, visit of President George W. Bush to the site of the previous day's terrorist attack on the Pentagon. *(DoD photo by R. D. Ward)*

▲

Army National Guard medic Sgt. Frank Ruffo shows the strain of seven straight days and nights of duty at Ground Zero in Manhattan. Ruffo, a member of New York's 101st Cavalry, spent most of his time working at the makeshift on-site morgue. *(U.S. Army photo)*

From left: Col. Andrew Leider, Col. Frank
Ombres and Lt. Col. Tom Newcomb, all New
York Army guardsmen, provide liaison with New
York City's Office of Emergency Management
for the recovery effort. *(Pete Murphy, AUSA News)*

From left, Pfc. Cory Coyne and Pfc. Mark Lupiani, New York Army guardsmen, patrol the perimeter around the World Trade Center site in cooperation with New York police. *(Pete Murphy, AUSA News)*

A New York Army guardsman checks a truck entering Manhattan, October 2001. Working with the New York police in the aftermath of the terrorist attacks, guardsmen check all vehicles heading into and out of Manhattan.

(Pete Murphy, AUSA News)

The American flag waves above the building
skeletons at Ground Zero, New York. *(Pete Murphy,
AUSA News)*

Pvt. Daniel Fox Jr., 54th Quartmaster Company (Mortuary Affairs), embraces his family after returning home to Fort Lee, Va., from assisting in the post-attack recovery mission at the Pentagon, September 2001. *(U.S. Army photo by Spc. Jamie Carson)*

Military District of Washington

Army National Guard

State Area Command,
New York Army National Guard

42d Infantry Division

U.S. Army Reserve

In the immediate post-attack weeks, Americans discovered new levels of cooperation among the armed services and civilian activities. The potential perils stimulated the growing teamwork.

President George W. Bush addressed a Joint Session of Congress and the American people on Sept. 20, 2001. He closed with these words: "Great harm has been done to us. We have suffered great loss. And in our grief and anger we have found our mission and our moment. Freedom and fear are at war. The advance of human freedom—the great achievement of our time, and the great hope of every time—now depends on us. Our nation —this generation— will lift a dark threat of violence from our people and our future. We will rally the world to this cause by our efforts, by our courage. We will not tire, we will not falter, and we will not fail."

Defending the Homeland

In the aftermath of 9/11, the cleanup operations at Ground Zero in New York City and the Pentagon produced extraordinary results achieved through widespread cooperation among disparate agencies and organizations.

Throughout the nation, people took homeland security and defense seriously. The defense establishment initiated and responded to continued needs for teamwork and coordination at local, state and federal levels. Existing strong relationships among active duty units at military bases and nearby communities grew more robust and expanded regionally. Collectively, the homeland security activities of the war on terrorism became known as Operation Noble Eagle.

State governors called up National Guard units to bolster security. In addition, the federal government began a partial mobilization of National Guard and reserve individuals and units for immediate and potential operations. Air travelers became accustomed to seeing National Guard soldiers reinforcing security at more than 400 airports. Guardsmen worked with United States Customs officers to enhance security at entry points.

◀

Departing New York for a one-day break from emergency duty, Spc. David C. Mahoney, a New York Army guardsman, posts his poem about his experiences in Lower Manhattan on a remembrance board at Grand Central Station, October 2001. *(Pete Murphy, AUSA News)*

Secretary of Defense Donald H. Rumsfeld promised to have the damaged wedge of the Pentagon rebuilt within one year of the attack. The restoration was completed and dedicated on Sept. 11, 2002.

By mid-2003, the Defense Department reported that call-ups for all services totaled more than 220,000 guardsmen and reservists. Of that number, more than 146,000 were Army reservists and guardsmen. Communities nationwide from Abbeville, Ala., to Rock Springs, Wyo., felt the impact of the call-ups. For example, the city of Boone, Iowa (population 12,800) saw 166 guardsmen mobilized. From Peru, Ill. (population 8,835), 119 U.S. Army reservists were called to federal service. Lt. Gen. James R. Helmly, Chief, Army Reserve, defined the Army's reliance on its reserve components. He said in 2003, "What was once a 'force in reserve' has become a full partner across the spectrum of operations to satisfy the demand and need for Army Reserve soldiers and units around the world."

Virginia Army National Guard Spc. Geoffrey
Briggs of the 229th Military Police Company
from Chesapeake, Va., stands guard in a pas-
senger concourse at Ronald Reagan Washington
National Airport after the facility opened for the
first time in three weeks. *(U.S. Army photo by*
Sgt. 1st Class Eric Wedeking, National Guard Bureau)

Cast and crew of the U.S. Army Soldier
Show march to their own cadence in the
patriotic finale of their show in autumn
2001. The show, an activity of the
Community and Family Support Center,
continued its tour after the attacks of
Sept. 11, 2001, bringing smiles and tears
to audiences totaling more than 100,000.
(U.S. Army photo by Douglas Ide)

Civic leaders in New York's "North Country"
acknowledge a special bond between
their communities and Fort Drum. Robert F.
Hagemann III, Jefferson County administra-
tor, left, Mary Courriveau, assistant city
manager of Watertown, and attorney Keith
Caughlin value the relationship with the
Army. *(John Grady, AUSA News)*

First Lady Laura Bush, left, Lt. Gen. John Van Alstyne, center, and President George W. Bush, right, join a joint-service chorus and thousands of flag-waving Pentagon personnel in singing "God Bless America" during a memorial ceremony at the Pentagon Oct. 11, 2001. *(U.S. Army photo by Staff Sgt. Michael Rautio)*

From left: Secretary of Defense Donald H. Rumsfeld and Secretary of the Army Thomas E. White take questions from reporters at the Pentagon on Oct. 11, 2001. Rumsfeld and White discussed homeland defense, the air campaign being directed against the al Qaeda terrorist organization and the military capability of the Taliban regime in Afghanistan. *(DoD photo by R. D. Ward)*

Reconstruction of the Pentagon continues nearly around-the-clock as construction crews pour concrete for floors and walls on Feb. 6, 2002, to replace those damaged in the Sept. 11, 2001, terrorist attack on the building. *(DoD photo by Grant Greenwalt)*

The Pentagon's America's Heroes Memorial is dedicated to the 184 victims killed in the Sept. 11, 2001, terrorist attack on the Pentagon. The names of the victims are engraved on black acrylic panels inside the horseshoe-shaped memorial. A book containing photographs and biographies of each of the victims is at the center of the memorial under the "United in Memory" seal. *(DoD photo by Helene C. Stikkel)*

An inscribed plaque listing the 184 victims of the Sept. 11, 2001, terrorist attack on the Pentagon is among items in a bronze dedication capsule placed behind the last limestone block in the Pentagon's repaired outer west wall on June 11, 2002. *(DoD photo by Gerry J. Gilmore)*

▲

Soldiers of the 363d Military Police Company undergo weapons qualification with M-249 squad automatic weapons at Fort Dix, N.J., to prepare for security duties at Tobyhanna Army Depot, Pa. The 363d is a U.S. Army Reserve unit from Grafton, W.Va. The unit was called to active duty as part of the partial mobilization of reserve components that began in September 2001.

(U.S. Army photo by Anthony J. Ricchiazzi)

▲
A truck driver in the Maine Army National Guard's 1136th Transportation Company moves out after being mobilized for the war against terrorism. He deployed from Maine on Feb. 25, 2002. *(Photo by Sgt. Bob Haskell, National Guard Bureau)*

▲
Soldiers of the 349th Chemical Company decontaminate a Seattle area resident in the homeland defense TOPOFF2 exercise, May 20, 2003. *(U.S. Army photo by Spc. Kelly A. Rinehart)*

▲
Spc. Michael Scott of the Vermont National Guard stands near the small Morses Line, Vt., border entry port. Vermont National Guard soldiers on federal active duty with Task Force Sentinel support the U.S. Customs Service and Immigration and Naturalization Service at eight ports of entry on the Canadian border.

(Dennis Steele, ARMY Magazine)

◄
Spc. Amanda Collins repairs an OH-58D helicopter. She is a member of the Vermont Reconnaissance and Aerial Interdiction Detachment, a team of Vermont-based National Guard aviators on active federal service to support the U.S. Border Patrol by flying surveillance missions along the U.S.-Canadian border.

(Dennis Steele, ARMY Magazine)

▲

Staff Sgt. Shawn Cheney of the Vermont
National Guard inspects a truck's cab while
supporting the U.S. Customs Service at Highgate
Springs, Vt. *(Dennis Steele, ARMY Magazine)*

President George W. Bush speaks at the Sept. 11, 2002, memorial service at the rebuilt Pentagon. More than 13,000 people attended the service to remember those who lost their lives one year earlier when terrorists crashed a commercial airliner into the building.

(DoD photo by Larry McTighe)

Secretary of the Army Thomas E. White speaks to Reserve soldiers going through the Soldier Readiness Process at Fort Campbell, Ky., about their indispensable role in today's Army.

(U.S. Army photo by Sgt. Reeba Critser)

Master Sgt. Gary L. Beaver, Virginia Army guardsman, and his wife Linda tell members of Congress about their experience in mobilizing. Beaver, a police officer in Fairfax County, Va., deployed to Afghanistan for Operation Enduring Freedom. *(John Grady, AUSA News)*

United States Northern Command

U.S. Army Special Forces Group (Airborne)

Homeland defense evolved into enduring and high-priority missions for the United States Army and its sister services. Concurrently, the need to find and eliminate terrorist organizations became an urgent global requirement.

Many nations suffered terrorist atrocities before the horrific events of 9/11 in the United States. In addition to protecting the homeland against terrorism, the U.S. government reinforced the coalition to wage a global war against terrorists and their supporters. The United Nations Security Council adopted resolutions for international cooperation to combat terrorism.

The U.S. government determined that the al Qaeda terrorist organization conducted the attacks on 9/11. It also concluded that al Qaeda received refuge and support from the Taliban government of Afghanistan. The Taliban defied the United Nations. Direct action was required.

The Coalition Strikes

Preparations for smashing the al Qaeda terror organization and the Taliban regime sheltering and supporting it developed rapidly. Nations bordering Afghanistan such as Pakistan, Uzbekistan and Tajikistan cooperated in the buildup by the coalition led by the United States and Great Britain. Other nations granted over-flight rights for aerial movement by coalition forces. The United States Navy moved aircraft carrier battle groups and supporting ships into position. United States Air Force expeditionary wings flew into designated bases in nations around Afghanistan and Iraq.

The forces to deliver the assault against ter-rorism stood ready. In Kuwait and elsewhere in the Gulf region, other forces came to a high state of alert to deter Saddam Hussein of Iraq from lashing out against his neighbors.

President George W. Bush pulled the trig-ger. He addressed the nation and the world in midday on Oct. 7, 2001: "On my orders, the United States military has begun strikes

against al Qaeda terrorist training camps and military installations of the Taliban regime in Afghanistan. These carefully targeted actions are designed to disrupt the use of Afghanistan as a terrorist base of operations, and to attack the military capability of the Taliban regime." Operation Enduring Freedom got under way.

Swiftly and efficiently, members of the Army Rangers, Special Forces, and units of the multi-service Special Operations Command joined advance parties already on the ground in Afghanistan. They demonstrated extraordinary flexibility and adaptability in carrying out the missions assigned, such as linking up and mak-ing alliances with tribal groups. Aircraft of the United States Air Force and Navy provided air power in support of the activities on the ground. To give just three examples, they smashed resistance encountered by the special operators, they delivered logistical support to friendly forces, and they parachuted humanitar-ian rations to needy Afghanis.

As Operation Enduring Freedom developed momentum, additional forces from Great Britain, Australia and New Zealand joined in the campaign.

◀

Kuwait, November 2001, Sgt. John Newman, a Company A, 1st Battalion, 5th Cavalry Regiment Bradley commander, checks the perimeter while on security detail. An Abrams tank backs him up.
(Dennis Steele, ARMY Magazine)

1st Sgt. Edward Spaulding, Company A, 1st
Battalion, 5th Cavalry Regiment, on station
in Kuwait. *(Dennis Steele, ARMY Magazine)*

Sgt. Sean Heath of the 251st Cargo Transfer Company, 21st Theater Support Command, cinches a strap on a pallet that will be parachuted into Afghanistan. *(Dennis Steele, ARMY Magazine)*

Tiger 2 reconnaissance team of
Headquarters and Headquarters Company,
2d Battalion, 187th Infantry Regiment.
(Dennis Steele, ARMY Magazine)

U.S. Army Special Forces troops ride horseback
as they work with members of the Northern
Alliance in Afghanistan during Operation
Enduring Freedom on Nov. 12, 2001. *(DoD photo)*

Maj. Don Bolduc, standing, Capt. Hank Smith, seated left, and Lt. Col. Dave Fox, seated right, brief
Gul Agha Sharzai, the governor of newly liberated
Kandahar Province, on Dec. 10, 2001. Smith's team
had secured the Kandahar Airfield on Dec. 6. The
briefing by the officers of the 5th Special Forces
Group (Airborne) covered the plan to make the city
of Kandahar stable, safe and secure. Five days later,
the Army Special Forces teams began escorting
U.S. Marine units into the area. *(U.S. Army photo)*

Army Rangers of the 75th Ranger Regiment who had parachuted into Afghanistan in October returned to Fort Benning, Ga., on Dec. 7, 2001. Col. Joseph Votel, the regiment's commander, told the crowd that "there is no greater feeling for a Ranger than to know his country is behind him—100 percent and then some." *(U.S. Army photo by Pvt. Brian Trapp)*

U.S. Army AH-64 Apache and UH-60 Black Hawk helicopters, operating from U.S. Navy aircraft carriers such as the USS *Kitty Hawk*, fly Special Forces troops more than 400 miles from the Arabian Sea into Taliban-controlled Afghanistan early in Operation Enduring Freedom. *(DoD photo by Joint Shipboard Helicopter Integration Process Office)*

Pfc. Daniel Cunningham writes a letter on a piece of cardboard from a ration box while Pvt. David Baker stands watch. Both are with Company A, 2d Battalion, 187th Infantry Regiment. *(Dennis Steele, ARMY Magazine)*

Army Chief of Staff Gen. Eric K. Shinseki speaks to soldiers of the 10th Mountain Division (Light Infantry) at a base camp in Uzbekistan on Thanksgiving Day, 2001. *(U.S. Army photo)*

Army Chief of Staff Gen. Eric K. Shinseki talks with Sgt.1st Class Ronnie Raikes before the State of the Union address on Jan. 29, 2002. Raikes, wounded in Afghanistan, sat with First Lady Laura Bush during the address. *(U.S. Army photo by Staff Sgt. Michael Rautio)*

Soldiers from the 4th Platoon, Company D, 2d Battalion, 187th Infantry Regiment, 101st Airborne Division (Air Assault), assemble for a photograph after returning from a patrol in Afghanistan.

(Dennis Steele, ARMY Magazine)

Vehicles from Task Force Rakkasan cross the desert of southern Afghanistan near Kandahar on a reconnaissance mission. *(Dennis Steele, ARMY Magazine)*

Pvt. Daniel Smith, Company D, 2d Battalion, 187th Infantry Regiment, wields a shovel to put the finishing touches on a fighting position for his anti-tank Humvee. *(Dennis Steele, ARMY Magazine)*

1st Cavalry Division

10th Mountain Division (Light Infantry)

101st Airborne Division
(Air Assault)

U.S. Special Operations Command

U.S. Army Special Operations Command

75th Ranger Regiment

On Jan. 17, 2002, Secretary of State Colin Powell officiated as the United States Embassy in Kabul, Afghanistan, reopened after being closed since 1989.

Among the topics in his State of the Union Address on Jan. 29, 2002, President Bush reported on Operation Enduring Freedom.

He said, "Our progress is a tribute to the spirit of the Afghan people, to the resolve of our coalition, and to the might of the United States military. When I called our troops into action, I did so with complete confidence in their courage and skill. And tonight, thanks to them, we are winning the war on terror. The men and women of our Armed Forces have delivered a message now clear to every enemy of the United States: Even 7,000 miles away, across oceans and continents, on mountaintops and in caves— you will not escape the justice of this nation."

U.S. Army map

Multifaceted Campaign

The initial military activities of Operation Enduring Freedom in Afghanistan began with Special Operations Forces on the ground supported by air and naval elements. Before long, enemy combatants captured in the fighting were dispatched to a detainee compound at the United States Navy base at Guantanamo Bay, Cuba.

Larger ground units of the United States Army, Marine Corps, and coalition partners added power and flexibility to the campaign as it spread throughout Afghanistan in late 2001 and early 2002. The 10th Mountain Division (Light Infantry) and brigade task forces from the 101st Airborne Division (Air Assault) pursued and destroyed Taliban and al Qaeda terrorists into high mountain caves and parched desert lairs.

United States Army infantry units flew assault helicopters into remote landing zones and fought close up with their individual weapons. Army attack helicopters and strike aircraft of the United States Air Force, Marine Corps, Navy and Royal Air Force delivered on-call firepower to compensate for the lack of direct support artillery.

Night-vision technologies enabled individual soldiers to wage the war around the clock. Logistical support for combat operations and humanitarian activities flowed from around the world to the cities and remotest corners of Afghanistan. Soldiers learned to adapt and deal with varying tribal customs of their new Afghan allies.

Operation Anaconda, fought in March 2002 in the high mountains and narrow valleys of the Shah-e-Kot range of eastern Afghanistan, proved a model of joint and combined cooperation and flexibility. Coalition partners fused into smooth functioning fighting teams to carry out difficult missions against determined enemies in unforgiving terrain and weather.

Through the spring and summer of 2002, seasoned units rotated back to home stations in the United States. New units, such as task forces from the 82d Airborne Division, had been training for deployment. They landed in Afghanistan ready to fight and to continue the implacable pressure on remaining terrorist elements.

◀

Pvt. David Taylor of Company C, 2d Battalion, 187th Infantry Regiment, 101st Airborne Division (Air Assault), stands guard at Kandahar International Airport in Afghanistan during Operation Anaconda, March 2002. *(Dennis Steele, ARMY Magazine)*

▲

Bagram, Afghanistan, Feb. 28, 2002. Lt. Col. Ronald
Corkran, left, commander of the 1st Battalion, 187th
Infantry Regiment, 101st Airborne Division (Air Assault),
makes a point to Col. Francis J. Wiercinski, right, commander of Task Force Rakkasan, during a planning
session before Operation Anaconda. In the center
is Lt. Col. Paul Lacamera, commander of the 1st
Battalion, 87th Infantry Regiment, 10th Mountain
Division (Light Infantry). The commanders overlook
a model of the terrain involved. *(U.S. Army photo by
Sgt. David Marck Jr.)*

▲

Spc. Jerry Rhoades and Sgt. Aaron Moya, armament and electrician repairmen for AH-64A Apache helicopters, remove a maintenance apparatus from the front of an Apache of the 101st Aviation Regiment, 101st Airborne Division (Air Assault). The expert soldiers prepared the Apaches for participation in Operation Anaconda, March 2002. *(U.S. Army photo by Spc. George Allen)*

Company C, 4th Battalion, 31st Infantry Regiment, moves through the Afghan mountains.
(Dennis Steele, ARMY Magazine)

Soldiers conduct a dismounted patrol in Guantanamo Bay, Cuba, to provide security to the detainee compound. *(DoD photo by Chief Petty Officer John F. Williams, U.S. Navy)*

An Army reservist (and recent immigrant to the United States), who is fluent in several languages of the Southwest Asia region, serves at Guantanamo Bay, Cuba. He functions as translator and interrogator in the center holding detainees from Operation Enduring Freedom.
(U.S. Army photo by Sgt. 1st Class Susanne Aspley)

Operation Enduring Freedom

MPs from the 401st Military Police Company, III Corps, Fort Hood, Texas, serving at Guantanamo Bay Naval Base, Cuba. Back row, from left: Sgt. William Fike, Jr., Pfc. Andrew Grundhoffer and Sgt. Richard Manning. Front row, from left: Pfc. Barbara Evans and Sgt. James Scott. *(Dennis Steele, ARMY Magazine)*

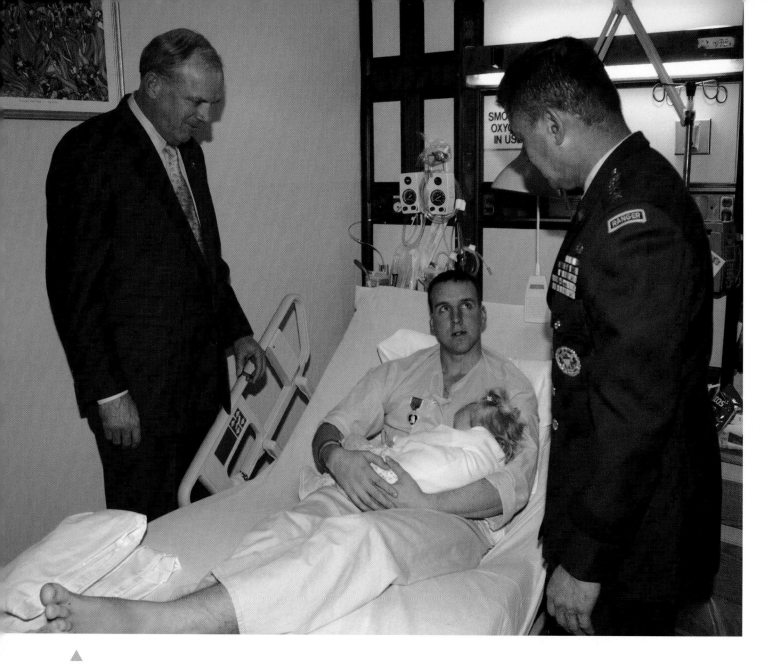

Sgt. Thomas D. Finch of Company C, 1st Battalion, 87th Infantry
Regiment, 10th Mountain Division (Light Infantry), Fort Drum,
N.Y., holds his daughter, Emily, at Walter Reed Army Medical
Center, Washington, D.C., in March 2002. Army Chief of Staff
Gen. Eric K. Shinseki, right, and Secretary of the Army Thomas E.
White, left, talk with Finch after presenting him with the Purple
Heart for wounds received during Operation Anaconda
in Afghanistan. (*U.S. Army photo by Staff Sgt. Michael Rautio*)

A soldier-made signpost stands in a tent city
at Bagram air base, Afghanistan. *(Dennis Steele,
ARMY Magazine)*

Sirkankel, Afghanistan. Soldiers of the 1st Battalion, 187th
Infantry Regiment, 101st Airborne Division (Air Assault),
scan the ridgeline for enemy forces during Operation
Anaconda. *(U.S. Army photo by Sgt. David Marck Jr.)*

1st Lt. Steve LaValle of the 41st Engineer Battalion places a demolition charge on a cache in the Afghan mountains during a mission with the 4th Battalion, 31st Infantry Regiment. *(Dennis Steele, ARMY Magazine)*

Soldiers of the 4th Battalion, 31st Infantry Regiment, shield themselves against the rotor wash of a CH-47 Chinook helicopter that is picking them up from a mission. *(Dennis Steele, ARMY Magazine)*

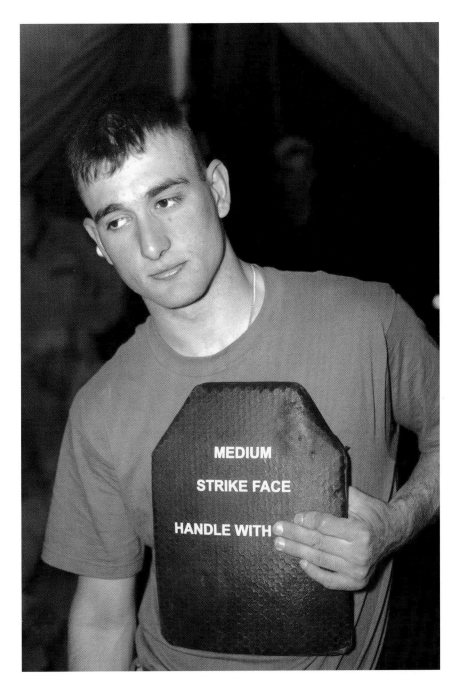

Pfc. Jason Ashline, of the 1st Battalion, 87th Infantry Regiment, 10th Mountain Division (Light Infantry), holds the body armor that protected him when he was shot during an intense firefight of Operation Anaconda, March 2002. A dent in the upper right-hand corner of the armor shows where a bullet failed to penetrate it. Ashline survived the battle unhurt.

(U.S. Army photo by Spc. Steven L. McGowan)

▲

Sgt. Maj. of the Army Jack L. Tilley converses with soldiers of the 101st Airborne Division (Air Assault) during his visit to Kandahar Airfield, Afghanistan, April 5, 2002. Tilley had a question-and-answer session with the soldiers. *(U.S. Army photo by Pfc. Christopher Stanis)*

▲

A soldier of the 1st Battalion, 187th Infantry Regiment, 101st Airborne Division (Air Assault), mans a .50-caliber machine gun during Operation Anaconda, March 2002. The battlefield is in eastern Afghanistan, south of Gardez in the Shah-e-Kot mountain range.

(U.S. Army photo by Sgt. David Marck Jr.)

A grenade explodes in a Ginger Valley cave and soldiers
of Company A, 4th Battalion, 31st Infantry Regiment,
rush to clear it. *(Dennis Steele, ARMY Magazine)*

A new recruit of the Afghan National Army is measured for his boot size (9-1/2R) during uniform issue at the Afghan National Army training site in Kabul,Afghanistan, on May 14, 2002. Approximately 150 U.S. Special Forces soldiers are deployed to Kabul to equip and train recruits of the new Afghan National Army in training cycles of approximately 10 weeks in duration. *(DoD photo by Staff Sgt. Kevin P. Bell, U.S. Army)*

▼

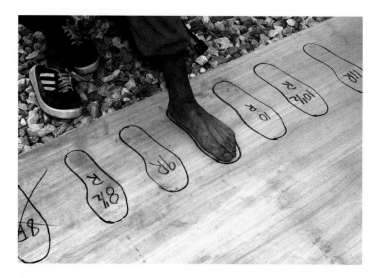

▲

From left: Afghan Interim Chairman Hamid Karzai and U.S. Army Maj. Gen. Franklin L. Hagenbeck talk with soldiers of Hagenbeck's 10th Mountain Division (Light Infantry) at Bagram Airfield, Afghanistan, on March 30, 2002. *(U.S. Army photo by Sgt. David Marck Jr.)*

Soldiers of the 10th Mountain Division (Light Infantry)
participating in Operation Anaconda prepare to dig
into fighting positions before sunset, March 4, 2002.

(U.S. Army photo by Sgt. David Marck Jr.)

Royal Marine Commandos from 45 Commando return
from Operation Ptarmigan to Bagram air base, Afghanistan,
aboard a U.S. Army CH-47 Chinook helicopter, April 18, 2002.
(UK Ministry of Defence photo by Tony Leather. Copyright British
Crown/Copyright Ministry of Defence)

Command Sgt. Maj. Mark Nielsen of the 187th Infantry Regiment (an element of Task Force Rakkasan), from the 101st Airborne Division (Air Assault) in Afghanistan during Operation Anaconda, March 2002. *(Dennis Steele, ARMY Magazine)*

From left: Spc. James Pittman, 421st Quartermaster (Rigger) Company, and German Army Cpl. Christian Hallmannsegger attach a parachute to a crate of supplies during Task Force Firepower's humanitarian aid missions in Afghanistan. *(U.S. Army photo by 21st TASCOM)*

Paratroopers from the 3d Battalion, 505th Parachute Infantry Regiment, 82d Airborne Division, exit a U.S. Air Force C-17 Globemaster transport at Kandahar Airfield, Afghanistan, on June 27, 2002. The paratroopers relieved the soldiers of Task Force Rakkasan of the 101st Airborne Division (Air Assault). *(U.S. Army photo by Pfc. Jason B. Baker)*

President George W. Bush salutes soldiers and families of Fort Drum, N.Y. He proclaimed, "When the 10th Mountain Division first arrived in Afghanistan, the Taliban was in power. When some of you left, the Taliban was in ruins and the Afghan people were liberated."
(U.S. Army photo by Glenn Wagner)

United States Army Element,
U.S. Central Command

United States Central Command

82d Airborne Division

United States Army Europe

By late March 2002, schools reopened in Afghanistan, validation of the winter and spring campaigns. United States Army Reserve units such as civil affairs, medical, veterinary, military police and engineers buttressed the combat accomplishments and fostered regeneration of the Afghan nation.

An Islamic Transitional Government came into being in June 2002 with Hamid Karzai elected as its president.

Secretary of the Army Thomas E. White lauded the performance of the soldiers of Operation Enduring Freedom. He summarized it this way to the Senate Armed Services Committee on March 6, 2003: "In the dead of winter, in a land-locked country, in the toughest terrain imaginable, they collapsed the Taliban regime and put al Qaeda on the run."

Transforming Afghanistan

United States Army soldiers campaigning in Operation Enduring Freedom demonstrated the highest standards of their profession. Soldiers at all levels exemplified the values of training and discipline and taking care of each other.

Army units, working in concert with other United States services and coalition partners, applied relentless force against terrorist enemies who flouted the laws of war. The soldiers employed force with precision to spare non-combatants while eradicating terrorists. Air assaults into mountain redoubts at altitudes above 14,000 feet tested the capabilities of men and machines. Soldiers battled with sand and heat while hunting terrorists in the dry desert regions. New technologies such as global positioning systems, night-vision devices and unmanned aerial vehicles aided soldiers in mission accomplishment. Essential elements of mission success included physical fitness and a commitment to duty and honor.

The pursuit of terrorists and their supporters continued without pause throughout 2002 and 2003. Concurrently, the United States Army and coalition partners paid attention to the noncombatants. Innocent victims of more than two decades of war and Taliban oppression found that coalition forces, working with the new Afghan government, understood their needs for the basic necessities of life such as food, shelter and medical care.

Engineers and civil affairs and medical and veterinary soldiers found—and surmounted—plenty of challenges in the cities and villages of Afghanistan. Partners from Australia, Canada, the Republic of Korea, New Zealand, Poland and others pitched in to help restore a society craving the simple things of life. Soldiers carried out both combat and humanitarian missions while being aware of, and respecting, cultural and tribal differences in the Afghan society.

The prospects of a new beginning for Afghanistan brightened with eradicating the Taliban regime and scattering the al Qaeda parasites from the country. Tangible evidence of progress showed in the building of healthcare clinics and schools. Highways were rebuilt and a new Afghan National Army came into being.

◀

U.S. Army CH-47 Chinook helicopters carry the load in Afghanistan. *(Dennis Steele, ARMY Magazine)*

A Chinook helicopter picks up a sling load of supplies at Bagram air base in Afghanistan to sustain units in the field. *(Dennis Steele, ARMY Magazine)*

The guidon of Company A, 2d Battalion, 187th Infantry Regiment, stands above the company's command post bunker at Kandahar air base, Afghanistan. *(Dennis Steele, ARMY Magazine)*

▷

Capt. Todd Fleming from the Army Reserve's 401st Civil Affairs Battalion, Rochester, N.Y., and an interpreter speak with local Afghan residents during a medical assistance mission. *(U.S. Army photo)*

▷

Soldiers from the Army Reserve 489th Civil Affairs Battalion of Knoxville, Tenn., inspect the progress being made on the construction of a new school in the Parwan Province of Afghanistan on Sept. 8, 2002. The soldiers are members of the Coalition/Humanitarian Liaison Cell, and are currently overseeing the construction of six schools, two bridges, a major tunnel and two fresh water pumps in the province. *(DoD photo by Staff Sgt. Derrick C. Goode, U.S. Air Force)*

▷

U.S. Army veterinary personnel treat goats in the village of Sayed, Afghanistan, on Nov. 3, 2002. Medical and veterinary personnel from the U.S., Republic of Korea and Australian armed forces provide free treatment as part of humanitarian assistance programs for the people of Afghanistan. *(DoD photo by Sgt. Albert Eaddy)*

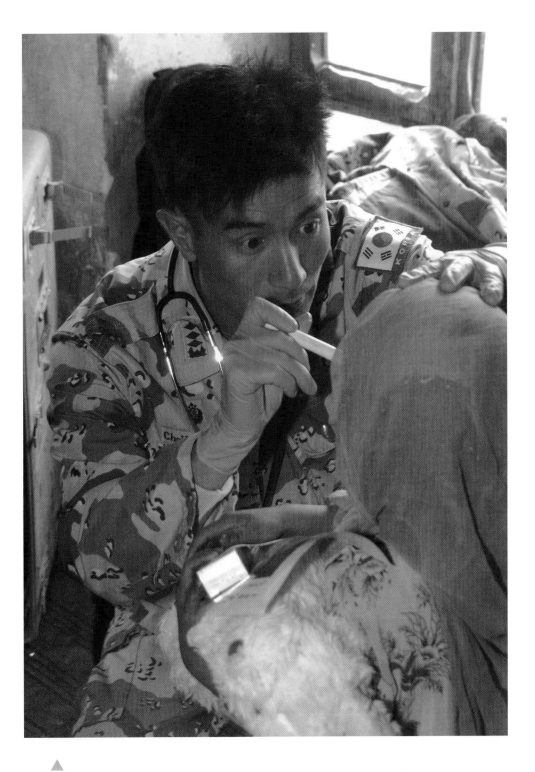

On Nov. 3, 2002, a doctor from the Republic of Korea based at Bagram Airfield gives medical and veterinarian aid to the village of Sayed, Afghanistan. *(U.S. Army photo by Sgt. Albert Eaddy)*

Staff Sgt. Charles Pearson of the 504th
Parachute Infantry leads his soldiers off the
landing zone and into the village of Zirgi,
Afghanistan. *(Dennis Steele, ARMY Magazine)*

▼

▲

A squad leader of Task Force Devil points out a
field of fire to one of his soldiers. *(Dennis Steele,
ARMY Magazine)*

Spc. Stephanie Pavliska, 82d Military Police
Company, participates in search team
operations in Zirgi, Afghanistan.
(Dennis Steele, ARMY Magazine)

President George W. Bush and First Lady Laura
Bush at Walter Reed Army Medical Center,
Washington, D.C., in January 2003 talk about
their visit with soldiers wounded in Afghanistan.

(U.S. Army photo by Brett McMillan)

Pfc. Anna Wear of the 82d Military Police
Company guards the door of a room where a
household's women have gathered. Only female
soldiers search or even see Afghan women.

(Dennis Steele, ARMY Magazine)

Staff Sgt. Charles Pearson and his squad of the 504th Parachute Infantry arrive at the pickup zone for exfiltration from Zirgi, Afghanistan.

(Dennis Steele, ARMY Magazine)

▲
Soldiers of Task Force Devil load aboard a Black Hawk helicopter during exfiltration from Zirgi, Afghanistan. *(Dennis Steele, ARMY Magazine)*

▲
A Task Force Devil soldier provides cover during an air assault into Landing Zone Owl in southeastern Afghanistan. *(Dennis Steele, ARMY Magazine)*

▲

Two soldiers with the 11th Signal Brigade's 504th Signal Battalion connect wire in an underground vault in Afghanistan. *(11th Signal Brigade photo)*

▲

Engineers, contractors, coalition forces and
Army National Guard soldiers worked with
the 11th Signal Brigade to wire the buildings
used by all services in Bagram, Afghanistan.
(11th Signal Brigade photo)

◄

Maj. Timothy Downs, center, of the Coalition Joint Civil Military Operation Task Force (CJCMOTF) and Lt. Col. Robert Sindler, right, also with CJCMOTF, meet with members of the Polish Humanitarian Organization at The Association for the Cultural Revival of Children and Youth in Afghanistan on Jan. 1, 2003. *(U.S. Army photo by Cpl. Jeremy Colvin)*

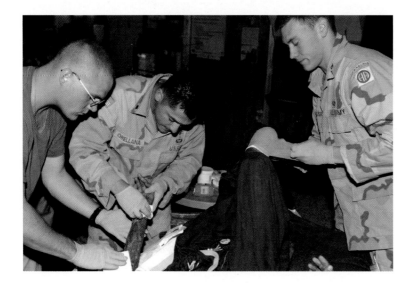

◄

From left: Pfc. Ryan Barrett, Company B, 2d Battalion, 504th Parachute Infantry Regiment combat medic, Spc. Rusvin Orellana, Company C (Medical), 307th Logistics Task Force combat medic, and 1st Lt. Steve Schmelzer, 307th Logistics Task Force registered nurse, treat an Afghan for extensive wounds caused by a land mine. *(U.S. Army photo by Spc. Jim Wagner)*

Capt. Michael Gonzalez of Company D, 1st Battalion, 504th Parachute Infantry Regiment, 82d Airborne Division, examines an old field rifle during Operation Valiant Strike on March 19, 2003. The rifle belonged to one of the villagers from the village of Patak in Kandahar Province, Afghanistan. *(U.S. Army photo by Staff Sgt. Leopold Medina Jr.)*

▶

A paratrooper of the 504th Parachute Infantry Regiment, 82d Airborne Division, emerges from searching the rooms of a compound in the village of Patak in Kandahar Province, Afghanistan, during Operation Valiant Strike, on March 19, 2003.

(U.S. Army photo by Staff Sgt. Leopold Medina Jr.)

▲

Paratroopers of the 82d Airborne Division set up their 105 mm howitzer to provide supporting fire for the 504th Parachute Infantry Regiment in Kandahar Province, Afghanistan, during Operation Valiant Strike on March 19, 2003.

(U.S. Army photo by Staff Sgt. Leopold Medina Jr.)

Staff Sgt. Richard Caldwell, assigned
to the 450th Civil Affairs Battalion, 82d
Airborne Division, in the Kohi Sofi region
of Afghanistan, March 2003. *(U.S. Army
photo by Sgt. 1st Class Milton H. Robinson)*

Paratroopers of the 505th Parachute Infantry
Regiment, 82d Airborne Division, take a break
after climbing the rugged mountain features
in the Kohi Sofi region of Afghanistan. *(U.S.
Army photo by Sgt. 1st Class Milton H. Robinson)*

A paratrooper of the 505th Parachute Infantry
Regiment, 82d Airborne Division, provides
security while the unit searches for a large
cache of weapons in the Kohi Sofi region of
Afghanistan, March 2003. *(U.S. Army photo by
Sgt. 1st Class Milton H. Robinson)*

Paratroopers of the 2d Battalion, 505th
Parachute Infantry Regiment, 82d Airborne
Division, debark from a CH-47 Chinook helicopter at Bagram Airfield. The paratroopers
conducted searches for weapon caches in
the mountains of Afghanistan near Kohi Sofi.

(U.S. Army photo by Sgt. Vernell Hall)

▲

Operation Resolute Strike, Sangin,
Afghanistan. Paratroopers of the 3d Battalion,
504th Parachute Infantry Regiment, 82d
Airborne Division task force, escort an Afghan
suspect to a CH-47 Chinook helicopter on
April 9, 2003. The task force conducted the
mission to gain intelligence on an ambush
of U.S. forces and to deny sanctuary and
weapons to anti-coalition forces.

(U.S. Army photo by Spc. Jim Wagner)

Sgt. Maj. of the Army Jack L. Tilley (in the hatch) receives instructions on driving a Soviet tank in Asadabad, Afghanistan, from Sgt. 1st Class Touw, Company D, 2d Battalion, 505th Parachute Infantry Regiment, 82d Airborne Division. *(82d Airborne Division photo by Master Sgt. Pam Smith)*

Kandahar, Afghanistan, May 14, 2003. A Polish officer watches vehicles line up for movement as a convoy from Kandahar Airfield to Kabul, the capital of Afghanistan. The convoy is to gather information to assist the Road Rebuilding Project in Afghanistan. *(U.S. Army photo by Sgt. Vernell Hall)*

III Corps

XVIII Airborne Corps

Back home in the United States, family readiness programs proved to be a critical element of combat power. These programs helped soldiers and their families through all stages of deployment. Family readiness programs addressed topics such as establishing lines of communication among units and families, setting up means for soldiers to keep in touch with families, assistance in financial planning and counseling, and operation of child and youth programs.

President George W. Bush said of Operation Enduring Freedom on Oct. 11, 2002: "We've seen in Afghanistan that the road to freedom can be hard; it's a hard struggle. We've also seen in Afghanistan that the road to freedom is the only one worth traveling. Any nation that sacrifices to build a future of liberty will have the respect, the support, and the friendship of the United States of America."

Buildup for Battle

While operations in Afghanistan continued, a new set of coalition forces was building up under the leadership of the United States of America. Its purpose: to deter aggression by the Saddam Hussein regime in Iraq and to take action against Iraq if directed. United States Central Command, already experienced at coalition operations, took on the tasks of planning and preparing for action.

Exceptional preparatory measures were necessary in case coalition forces were called upon to act. In the decade following the Desert Storm campaign, the United States armed forces had established forward bases and stockpiles of equipment and supplies in Kuwait and elsewhere in the Persian Gulf region. United States Army, Marine, Navy and Air Force units had rotated throughout the region for training for several years. However, should action be required against Iraq, more equipment would be needed for the forces tagged for the tasks.

If war came, it would be the first war fought using prepositioned equipment. An extraordinary sealift and airlift endeavor to place the necessary stocks in position began in the autumn of 2002 and continued well into the first half of 2003. Concurrently, active Army and reserve component units in the continental United States and in Europe received alert notices and began preparations for deployment. The Army Materiel Command (AMC) compiled data on the magnitude of the prepositioning enterprise. For example, 1.2 million tons of equipment needed to be moved more than 8,000 miles. AMC stated the items needed to be "the right stuff at the right time, in the right place, and in the right sequence." The Tank-automotive and Armaments Command, a subordinate command of AMC, shipped more than 67,000 spare parts worth more than $200 million during the period December 2002 to March 2003. The spares joined more than 16,000 wheeled vehicles and close to 700 armored vehicles prepositioned and ready for action.

◄

Shipping out. Spc. Brandon Bean hauls his baggage to the cargo hoist of the USNS *Yano* at a Charleston, S.C., military terminal. Bean, of the 3d Infantry Division (Mechanized), was among a group of more than 20 soldiers from various units who sailed aboard the *Yano* to check and safeguard military cargo for U.S. Central Command until it reached its destination.

(Dennis Steele, ARMY Magazine)

Vehicles roll up ramp of USNS *Yano* at Charleston, S.C., military terminal to begin the ocean voyage to the Persian Gulf region. *(Dennis Steele, ARMY Magazine)*

▶ Clark Chambers, the cargo operations chief of the 841st Transportation Battalion, Military Traffic Management Command, oversees the loading of the USNS *Yano*. *(Dennis Steele, ARMY Magazine)*

Military Traffic Management Command (MTMC) operations on an average day include:

6,550 individual shipments moving by truck, rail, barge or pipeline.

426 shipments of arms, ammunition or explosives.

1,596 ocean containers in transit.

50 ongoing stevedore and related terminal services under contract.

25 operations occurring at 25 seaports around the world.

597 MTMC personnel—civilian employees, reserve component and active duty military—deployed to support operations. *(Source: MTMC)*

▲ Michael Moody, the force protection officer for the 841st Transportation Battalion, watches as vehicles go up the USNS *Yano's* stern ramp at the Charleston, S.C., military terminal. Force protection for a ship-loading operation requires multiservice involvement. In the case of the Yano, the Navy guarded land approaches while the Coast Guard protected the water approaches. *(Dennis Steele, ARMY Magazine)*

Near Mannheim, Germany, a Humvee is lowered into the hold of a barge for river transport to a seaport en route to the Gulf. *(Dennis Steele, ARMY Magazine)*

▲

Kristine Sports, a marine cargo specialist in the 841st Transportation Battalion's operations section, calculates cargo space aboard the USNS *Yano*. *(Dennis Steele, ARMY Magazine)*

▶

What's for chow? A soldier of the Royal Irish Regiment tucks into a U.S. Army Meal, Ready-to-Eat during a lull in the zeroing of personal weapons on the 25-meter range in Kuwait in preparation for operations in Iraq. *(UK Ministry of Defence photo by WO2 Giles Penfound. Copyright British Crown /Copyright Ministry of Defence)*

▲

Spc. Henry Lacks squeezes past railcar side
posts as his unit, the 1st Battalion, 26th Infantry
Regiment, 1st Infantry Division (Mechanized),
loads vehicles for deployment to the Gulf.
(Dennis Steele, ARMY Magazine)

▲

Experts at Letterkenny Munitions Center, Pa.,
prepare containers full of Multiple Launch
Rocket System pods for shipment to Kuwait.
From left: Ron Wyrick, Denny Gipe and Paul
Butterball. *(U.S. Army photo by Ralph Peters)*

▲

Two roll-on/roll-off ships pass in the port of Corpus Christi, Texas, with cargo of the 4th Infantry Division (Mechanized), late January 2003. MV *Cape Taylor* (approaching bridge) passes MV *Cape Texas* at City Dry Cargo Dock #9. The U.S. Army Military Traffic Management Command planned and supervised the loading, and contract civilian longshoremen conducted it. The ships are maintained by the Maritime Administration for the Navy's Military Sealift Command. When activated, they arrive at the port of embarkation in four days or less.

(U.S. Transportation Command photo)

MV *Cape Texas*, a roll-on/roll-off ship of the
Navy's Military Sealift Command, encounters
choppy seas in the Mediterranean. It is en route
to the theater of operations with equipment of
the 4th Infantry Division (Mechanized).
(U.S. Transportation Command photo)

An M88A2 Hercules heavy equipment
recovery vehicle of the 4th Infantry
Division (Mechanized) debarks at Kuwait
on April 3, 2003. The vehicle made its ocean
voyage aboard the Navy's Military Sealift
Command vessel MV *Cape Victory* from
Corpus Christi, Texas. *(U.S. Army photo by
David Josar)*

Kuwait, March 3, 2003. Battalion Pipe Major
Alister Duffy plays the bagpipes for U.S. Marines
after an armor recognition class given by the
British Army. *(U.S. Marine Corps photo by
Sgt. Paul L. Anstine II)*

▲
Pfc. Charles Guillory of Arizona keeps watch under a full moon during exercises at dusk in the Kuwait desert Nov. 19, 2002. About 10,000 U.S. troops engaged in exercises 50 kilometers from the Iraqi border. *(U.S. Army photo, ARCENT)*

▲

Soldiers at Fort Bragg, N.C., attend an Army
Community Service class on managing their
personal finances in preparation for deployment.

(U.S. Army photo by Susan Spitalny)

A field artillery soldier from the 3d Infantry Division (Mechanized) guides a self-propelled 155 mm howitzer during a "refuel on the move" exercise in Kuwait, Nov. 19, 2002. *(U.S. Army photo, ARCENT)*

▲

Anastasia Kakel, center, family readiness coordinator for the 7th Transportation Group at Fort Eustis, Va., is flanked by Urana Stanley, left, a readiness volunteer, and Sgt. Heather Christian. Family readiness groups enhance the bonds between families and the Army. *(John Grady, AUSA News)*

The Family Readiness Center at Fort Stewart,
Ga., during a rare quiet moment in March 2003.

(*U.S. Army photo by Victoria Palmer*)

▲

An AH-64 Apache attack helicopter of the 101st Airborne Division (Air Assault) is moved to an assembly area at a port in the Gulf region on March 8, 2003, after a month-long journey from Fort Campbell, Ky., by air and sea. Movement control teams from U.S. Army Europe coordinated the arrival port operations. *(U.S. Army photo by Sgt. Ronald Mitchell)*

Broadcast programming. A member of the U.S. Army's 4th Psychological Operations Group (POG) edits an audio product received through the Deployable Audio Production System. Operators from the 4th POG and the U.S. Air Force's 193d Special Operations Wing broadcast television and radio programming that allows the U.S. to communicate directly to the Iraqi people.
(U.S. Navy photo by Photographer's Mate 1st Class Aaron Ansarov)

◀

Ajax, a military police dog used by Special Forces during Operation Iraqi Freedom, bares his teeth and tries to attack an onlooker, March 20, 2003. *(U.S. Navy photo by Photographer's Mate 2nd Class Alex C. Witte)*

Artillerymen of the 320th Field Artillery
Regiment, 101st Airborne Division (Air
Assault), fire a high explosive round from
their 105 mm howitzer at Udairi Range,
Kuwait. The exercises prepare the crews
to provide accurate combat fire support.

(U.S. Army photo by Spc. Robert Woodward)

U.S. Marine Corps Maj. Gen. Robert R. Blackman Jr., standing, chief of staff for the Coalition Forces Land Component Command (CFLCC), talks with CFLCC logistical officers following the morning's battle update assessment in the Coalition Operations and Intelligence Center.
(U.S. Army photo by Sgt. 1st Class David K. Dismukes)

▼

▲

Vehicles of the 3d Brigade Combat Team, 101st Airborne Division (Air Assault), face north as the brigade prepares to roll into Iraq, March 21, 2003.
(U.S. Army photo by Spc. Robert Woodward)

U.S. service members work around the clock in the Coalition Operations and Intelligence Center (COIC) to monitor the ground war in Iraq on March 22, 2003. The COIC is the hub of operations for the Coalition Forces Land Component Command led by Lt. Gen. David D. McKiernan.

(U.S. Army photo by Sgt. 1st Class David K. Dismukes)

▼

Contractors with MPRI, an L-3 Company, set up live fire exercises for coalition forces in Kuwait. From left: Larry Word, Program Manager; Denny Marshburn, MasterGunner; and Bob Kovacic, Live Fire Coordinator, review plans for pre-combat training at Camp Doha, Kuwait, in January 2003. *(MPRI photo)*

▼

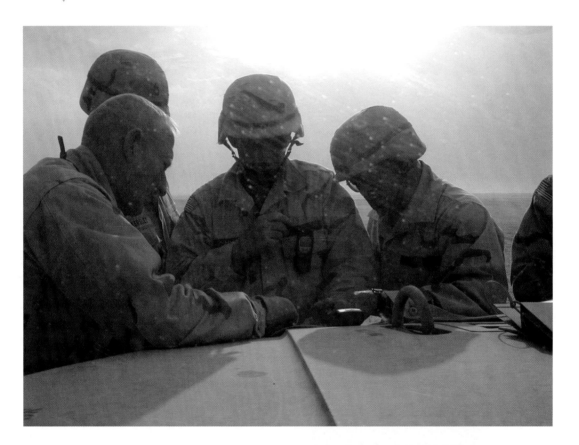

▲

Troops of Operation Iraqi Freedom must combat sandstorms as well as enemy forces. *(U.S. Army photo)*

▲

Sgt. A. Shevette of the 1st Battalion, 41st Infantry Regiment, 1st Armored Division, loads live ammunition for his M16 rifle before moving to a forward position in northern Kuwait on March 12, 2003.
(U.S. Army photo by Sgt. Igor Paustovski)

1st Infantry Division (Mechanized)

1st Armored Division

3d Infantry Division (Mechanized)

4th Infantry Division (Mechanized)

V Corps

Third Army

By early March 2003, major coalition combat forces of land, sea and air stood ready throughout the Persian Gulf region. Land force units including the United States Army's 3d Infantry Division (Mechanized) and the 1st Armored Division, the 1st Marine Expeditionary Force of the United States Marine Corps, plus British, Australian and other elements reached a peak of readiness.

Diplomatic initiatives by the United States and Great Britain at the United Nations occupied much of the fall and winter of 2002–2003. In October 2002, a unanimous U.N. Security Council passed Resolution 1441 holding Iraq in "material breach" of earlier U.N. resolutions. By early March 2003, British and U.S. patience with Iraq's noncompliance ran out and a March 17 deadline was announced. The deadline came and went. The coalition issued another ultimatum on March 17, stating that the Saddam Hussein regime had 48 hours (until March 19) to leave Iraq or face serious consequences.

Speed and Power Prevail

President George W. Bush announced the start of Operation Iraqi Freedom to the nation on the evening of March 19, 2003. He said, "My fellow citizens, at this hour, American and coalition forces are in the early stages of military operations to disarm Iraq, to free its people and to defend the world from grave danger."

As the president spoke, Special Operations Forces performed covert missions within Iraq. Coalition air and naval forces delivered precision air strikes against key Iraqi leadership and command and control targets. On ships and ashore, amphibious and ground fighting units checked their readiness for combat.

President Bush addressed them specifically. He said, "To all the men and women of the United States Armed Forces now in the Middle East, the peace of a troubled world and the hopes of an oppressed people now depend on you. That trust is well placed."

He continued, "The enemies you confront will come to know your skill and bravery. The people you liberate will witness the honorable and decent spirit of the American military. In this conflict, America faces an enemy who has no regard for conventions of war or rules of morality."

On March 20, coalition ground forces surged from Kuwait into Iraq along two major axes. The 3d Infantry Division (Mechanized) formed the core of the western axis, racing northwestward across the desert toward Baghdad. The 1st Marine Expeditionary Force and British regiments surged through the coastal region and past Basrah to approach Baghdad from the southeast. Coalition naval units opened seaborne approaches. Speed was essential to the success of the United States Central Command's plan. The advance along both axes was inexorable, surprising and overwhelming Iraqi resistance with precision firepower from ground, air and sea. Exceptional maintenance training and performance kept the mechanized columns rolling. The northern front opened on March 26. The 173d Airborne Brigade made a night parachute assault onto an airfield at Bashur. Baghdad fell on April 9.

◀

An arm modeled on Saddam Hussein's holds one of the swords at the monument honoring Iraq's "victory" over Iran. The helmets spilling from the net were taken from Iranian dead on the battlefields.

(Dennis Steele, ARMY Magazine)

▲

From left: Group Capt. Geoff Brown, Australia;
Gen. Tommy R. Franks, U.S. Central Command
commander-in-chief; Lt. Gen. T. Moseley, U.S. Air
Force; and Glenn Troy, Air Vice Marshal UK Air
Component, participate in a White House video-
conference at the start of Operation Iraqi
Freedom. *(CENTCOM photo by Navy Photographer
Gary P. Bonaccorso)*

◀

Previous page: Bradley Fighting Vehicles of the
3d Battalion, 15th Infantry Regiment, advance to
Baghdad through a sandstorm. *(Dennis Steele,
ARMY Magazine)*

▲
Mechanics of the 3d Battalion, 15th Infantry
Regiment, lower the engine of a Bradley
Fighting Vehicle for maintenance. Their skills
and dedication kept the mechanized columns
advancing with unprecedented speed and
power. *(Dennis Steele, ARMY Magazine)*

From left: Command Sgt. Maj. John Sparks, of the Coalition Forces Land Component Command (CFLCC), talks with CFLCC's senior intelligence officer Maj. Gen. James Marks and Lt. Gen. David D. McKiernan, CFLCC's commander. McKiernan noted on March 23, 2003, that the land force had moved as far in 32 hours as the forces did in 96 hours during Operation Desert Storm 12 years ago. *(U.S. Army photo by Sgt. 1st Class David K. Dismukes)*

U.S. Army Maj. Christine Edwards serves a meal for Iraqi civilians at the 86th Combat Support Hospital in south central Iraq. *(U.S. Army photo by Sgt. Kyran V. Adams)*

U.S. Army Brig. Gen. Robert Crear, commander
of the Southwest Division of the Corps of
Engineers, briefs international news media
at the Rumaila oil field, March 27, 2003.

(U.S. Army photo by Pfc. Mary Rose Xenikakis)

▲

A truckload of locals smile and cheer as they pass a U.S. convoy in the town of Basrah, Iraq, on April 12, 2003. *(DoD photo by Senior Airman Tammy L. Grider)*

▶

Flying to a night drop. Paratroopers from the 173d Airborne Brigade fill a U.S. Air Force C-17 Globemaster transport en route to the drop zone in Iraq. Several hundred "Sky Soldiers" of the brigade parachuted into Bashur, Iraq, on the night of March 26, 2003, helping to open a northern front in Operation Iraqi Freedom.

(U.S. Army photo)

▲

A jumpmaster of the 173d Airborne Brigade checks his paratroopers before they board an Air Force C-17 Globemaster transport. After a 4.5-hour flight from Aviano Air Base, Italy, the "Sky Soldiers" made a night drop into northern Iraq to seize the airfield at Bashur.

(U.S. Army photo by Spc. Cal Turner)

▲

Lt. Gen. David D. McKiernan, left, and Gen. Tommy R. Franks, U.S. Central Command commander-in-chief, confer on the tarmac at a forward operating airbase in Kuwait on April 7, 2003. *(CENTCOM photo by Navy Photographer Gary P. Bonaccorso)*

Army Special Operations MH-6 "Little Bird" helicopters lift off for a mission March 31, 2003, at a forward deployed location in southern Iraq. *(U.S. Air Force photo by Staff Sgt. Shane A. Cuomo)*

From left: Travis Richards, Julia Beal, Mikey Mayer and Scott McFatrich pack linked .50-caliber rounds into ammo cans at the Lake City Army Ammunition Plant in Independence, Mo., in March 2003 for shipment to the combat zone. *(U.S. Army photo by Darlene Young)*

U.S. Army Pfc. Sarah Weddle, a combat medic with the 546th Aerial Support Medical Company from Fort Hood, Texas, carries sandbags to hold down the field medical tent at an undisclosed location in Iraq on March 30, 2003. *(U.S. Air Force photo by Staff Sgt. Quinton T. Burris)*

U.S. Army Pfc. Breana McNanus conducts preventive maintenance checks and services on her vehicle in preparation for convoy operations on March 31, 2003, in south central Iraq. McNanus is a driver in the 82d Military Police Company, 82d Airborne Division. *(U.S. Army photo by Sgt. Kyran V. Adams)*

Ken Aten, an electronics mechanic at Tobyhanna Army Depot, monitors the power on the amplifier of an AN/TRC-170 troposcatter wideband communications system. He and three co-workers deployed to Kuwait in March 2003 to ensure that the systems of the 1st Marine Expeditionary Force operated at peak performance before the start of Operation Iraqi Freedom. *(U.S. Army photo by Michele Yeager)*

From left: Sgt. Brandi Harris and Maj. Tim
Haynie provide space communications capabilities in the Spectral Operations Resource Center
at As Sayliyah, Qatar. *(Army Space Command photo)*

▲

Traffic ceases at sunset at this U.S. Army
checkpoint on the Iraqi border, April 1, 2003.
(DoD photo by Senior Airman Tammy L. Grider)

◀

Col. Mike Mullins, Rock Island Arsenal commander, presents a commander's coin to
family child care provider Kathleen Berry
during a ceremony held on April 1, 2003,
on Arsenal Island, Ill. Berry was honored
for her selfless support for the child care
needs of military families who have a
deployed family member. She cares for
children from early morning until late at
night. *(U.S. Army photo by Nancy Reeves)*

U.S. Army Lt. Gen. David D. McKiernan, seated center, commander of the Coalition Forces Land Component Command, discusses battle plans with U.S. Marine Corps Lt. Gen. James Conway, left, commander of the 1st Marine Expeditionary Force, after the battle of An Nasseria, April 4, 2003. *(U.S. Army photo by Sgt. 1st Class David K. Dismukes)*

Soldiers follow in their Bibles as the Scripture is read during gospel service at Camp Virginia, Kuwait, on April 6, 2003. *(U.S. Army photo by Staff Sgt. Michelle Labrie)*

A fellow soldier returns gear to and congratulates Pvt. Christopher Nauman, who was wounded during the battle at Objective Curly south of Baghdad on April 7, 2003. Nauman insisted on keeping his shotgun with him as he was evacuated. En route to the aid station, an enemy soldier popped up and fired at the Americans. Nauman shot him. *(Dennis Steele, ARMY Magazine)*

Paratroopers of Company C, 2d Battalion, 325th Airborne Infantry Regiment, happily read long awaited mail on April 12, 2003, in Diawynia, Iraq. *(U.S. Army photo by Sgt. Kyran V. Adams)*

An AH-64 Apache attack helicopter with the 3d Aviation Regiment lands to rearm after destroying numerous surface-to-air threats in Baghdad, Iraq, April 11, 2003. *(U.S. Air Force photo by Staff Sgt. D. Myles Cullen)*

Abrams main battle tanks of the 3d Infantry Division (Mechanized) raise dust as they charge toward Baghdad. *(U.S. Army photo)*

The Scout Platoon of the 3d Battalion, 15th Infantry Regiment, honors the battalion's two soldiers and one journalist who died during Operation Iraqi Freedom as of April 12, 2003. Sgt. 1st Class John Marshall, the platoon sergeant of the scouts, was one of those who fell. *(Dennis Steele, ARMY Magazine)*

▲

U.S. Army CH-47 Chinook helicopters depart
on a dawn mission over Iraq in April 2003.

(U.S. Army photo, V Corps)

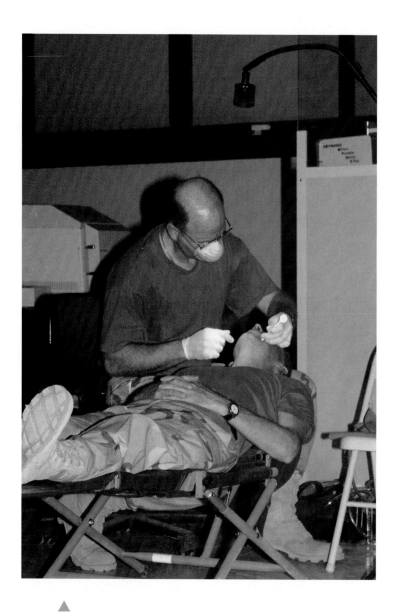

▲

A U.S. Army dentist provides expert care for a
soldier of V Corps somewhere in Iraq, April 2003.

(U.S. Army photo by Spc. Giovanni Lorente)

▲

Gen. Tommy R. Franks, commander of coalition forces, addresses Sgt. Lucas Goddard and Sgt. James Ward of the 327th Infantry Regiment, 101st Airborne Division (Air Assault), before presenting them with Bronze Stars for valor in combat.

(U.S. Army photo by Pfc. Joshua Hutcheson)

Soldiers of the 101st Airborne Division
(Air Assault) halt at a drainage ditch before
moving forward to their objective.

(U.S. Army photo by Sgt. Luis Lazzara)

Scouts of the 2d Armored Cavalry Regiment
display an orange recognition panel and the
American flag as they advance across Iraq.

(U.S. Army photo by Spc. Andrew Kosterman)

Gen. Tommy R. Franks, left, and his deputy,
Lt. Gen. John P. Abizaid, meet with Franks's
senior staff to discuss the progress of
Operation Iraqi Freedom at U.S. Central
Command's forward headquarters in Qatar.
General Abizaid succeeded General Franks
as commander in July 2003. *(CENTCOM photo
by Navy Photographer Gary P. Bonaccorso)*

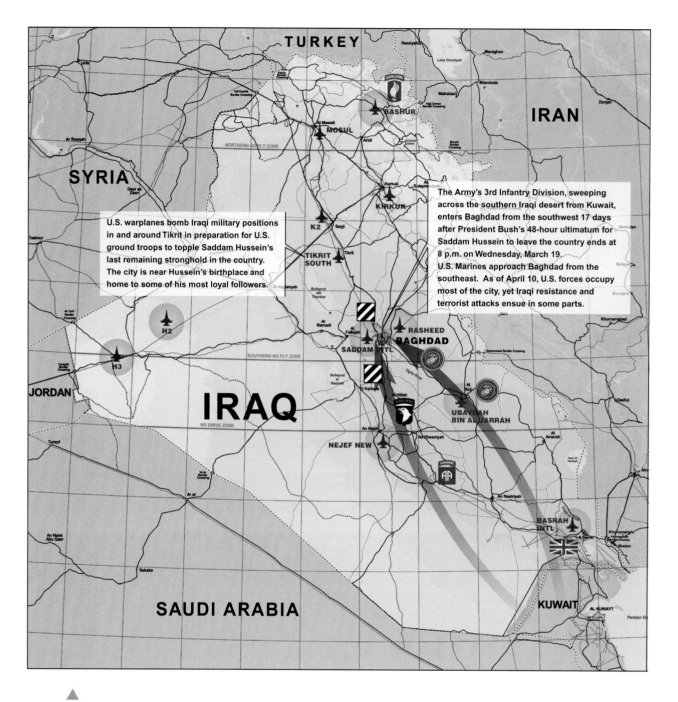

U.S. warplanes bomb Iraqi military positions in and around Tikrit in preparation for U.S. ground troops to topple Saddam Hussein's last remaining stronghold in the country. The city is near Hussein's birthplace and home to some of his most loyal followers.

The Army's 3rd Infantry Division, sweeping across the southern Iraqi desert from Kuwait, enters Baghdad from the southwest 17 days after President Bush's 48-hour ultimatum for Saddam Hussein to leave the country ends at 8 p.m. on Wednesday, March 19. U.S. Marines approach Baghdad from the southeast. As of April 10, U.S. forces occupy most of the city, yet Iraqi resistance and terrorist attacks ensue in some parts.

Operation Iraqi Freedom as of April 10, 2003.

(National Imagery and Mapping Agency map; graphics by AUSA News)

Staff Sgt. Chris Mize, a squad leader with 594th Transportation Company, makes a call to his family in the States from within a stone's throw of Iraq. Morale phones at Combat Support Center—Kuwait are provided voluntarily by a three-person team of Company B, 40th Signal Battalion.

(U.S. Army photo by Spc. M. William Petersen)

173d Airborne Brigade

2d Armored Cavalry Regiment

3d Armored Calvary Regiment

The fall of Baghdad constituted one milestone along the tough road to eventual victory in Iraq. Soldiers and Marines who had defeated regular Iraqi army units found themselves coping with widespread looting and random attacks from Saddam Hussein sympathizers and Baath Party remnants.

Aboard the aircraft carrier USS *Abraham Lincoln* on May 1, President Bush announced the end of major combat. He said, "In this battle, we have fought for the cause of liberty, and for the peace of the world. Our nation and our coalition are proud of this accomplishment—yet, it is you, the members of the United States military, who achieved it."

He continued, "We thank the Armed Forces of the United Kingdom, Australia and Poland, who shared in the hardships of war. We thank all the citizens of Iraq who welcomed our troops and joined in the liberation of their own country."

A Challenging Transition

Speed characterized the initial combat phase of Operation Iraqi Freedom from the opening shots to the fall of Baghdad on April 9. Additional United States Army combat units such as the 1st Infantry Division (Mechanized) and the 4th Infantry Division (Mechanized) had joined in the combat and continued to carry the fight to resistance throughout Iraq in April and May.

As more of the country came under coalition control, the tempo of operations shifted from fast-moving mechanized task forces to purposeful security operations and to restoring an economy debilitated by decades of oppression and corruption.

The combat campaign proceeded swiftly and with synchronized power. The immediate aftermath and the reconstruction of Iraq marched to a much slower and erratic beat.

The coalition campaign had applied force with precision to limit collateral damage to the nation's infrastructure and to minimize civilian casualties. However, because of decay, neglect,

looting and sabotage, the basic requirements for a functioning society were severely damaged. Food, water, gasoline and electricity as well as law and order were absent or minimal in cities large and small.

Soldiers trained and skilled in ground combat shifted their focus to building relationships with local communities through providing neighborhood security patrols and other essential services. Infantry soldiers and artillerymen and tankers reinforced rebuilding activities at schools and water points. Combat medics shored up neighborhood clinics and helped to reopen hospitals.

Once again, the men and women of the United States Army demonstrated their flexibility and adaptability to tackle non-combat problems. These included gaining an understanding of the different major religious and tribal groupings within Iraq. Or the challenges meant thwarting terrorist attacks on Americans and their vehicles and installations, or collaring looters.

The liberation of Iraq went according to plan. However, the occupation of post-Saddam Hussein Iraq remained, in mid-2003, a work in progress. The United States Army made major contributions to ensuring the success of all coalition activities.

Troops of the 2d Battalion, 69th Armor, 3d Infantry Division (Mechanized), travel the streets of northwest Baghdad on April 13, 2003. *(DoD photo by Sgt. Igor Paustovski)*

Vehicles of a U.S. Army armor column kick up dust as they traverse Baghdad International Airport on April 14, 2003. The airport is the primary base of operations for airlift of U.S. troops, cargo and humanitarian aid for Operation Iraqi Freedom. *(U.S. Air Force photo by Staff Sgt. Cherie A. Thurlby)*

Soldiers from the 3d Infantry Division (Mechanized) perform a reconnaissance security patrol near Yarmuk Hospital in Baghdad on April 14, 2003, while experts of the 96th Civil Affairs Battalion and Joint Task Force Four assess damage done by looting at the hospital. *(DoD photo by Staff Sgt. Jeremy T. Lock)*

A trooper of the 2d Armored Cavalry Regiment checks out a portrait of Saddam Hussein at An Najaf, Iraq, on April 11, 2003. The former Iraqi Army post in the city was cluttered with gear abandoned by fleeing Iraqi soldiers. *(U.S. Army photo by Spc. Andrew Kosterman)*

Iraqis protest against Saddam Hussein and for the United States (with a few conditions) during a nonviolent demonstration in front of the Palestine Hotel in downtown Baghdad, Iraq, on April 16, 2003. *(DoD photo by Staff Sgt. Kevin P. Bell, U.S. Army)*

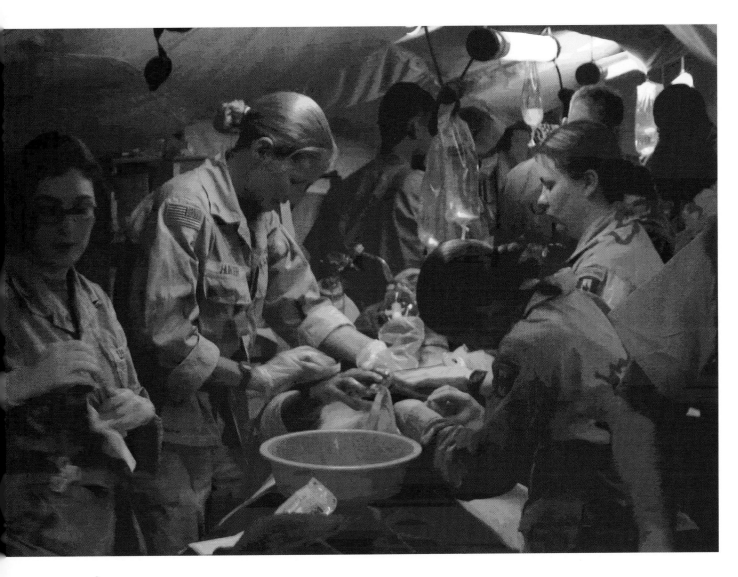

Staff members of the 86th Combat Support
Hospital, Camp Udairi, Kuwait, provide emergency medical care to a wounded soldier.
Medical facilities such as this are located
throughout Kuwait and Iraq to ensure quality
care is available to all soldiers. *(U.S. Army photo
by Lt. M. J. Oliveira)*

Sgt. Dave Marr of the 377th Theater Support Command's civil-military operations section provides potable drinking water to villagers near Tallil air base, Iraq, in mid-April 2003.

(U.S. Marine Corps photo by Sgt. Scott Whittington)

U.S. Army soldiers, British Royal Marines and
Iraqi civilians uncover train tracks at Az Zubayr,
Iraq, on April 18, 2003. The tracks run between
Basrah and the port of Umm Qasr. *(DoD photo by
Capt. Deborah Molnar)*

▲

Maj. Rodney King, a finance officer of the 82d Airborne Division, holds a stack of one hundred dollar bills. The cash is part of the estimated $650 million found hidden behind a fake wall at one of former Iraqi leader Saddam Hussein's palaces on April 19, 2003. The money is being transferred to a secure location where later it will be used in the reconstruction of Iraq.

(U.S. Army photo by Sgt. 1st Class David K. Dismukes)

President George W. Bush speaks with Chief
Warrant Officer David Williams and his family after
Easter service at Fort Hood's 4th Infantry Division
(Mechanized) Memorial Chapel. Apache pilots
Williams and Chief Warrant Officer Ronald Young Jr.
returned to Fort Hood, Texas, on April 19, 2003,
after 22 days as Iraqi prisoners of war. *(U.S. Army
photo by 1st Cavalry Division)*

Pvt. Joshua Johnson of the 4th Infantry Division (Mechanized), Fort Hood, Texas, secures the airport at Mosul, Iraq, on April 29, 2003. *(U.S. Air Force photo by Tech. Sgt. Stephen Faulisi)*

A flyover of Royal Australian Air Force F/A-18 Hornets concludes the observance of ANZAC Day at an air base in the Gulf region on April 25, 2003. The ceremonies commemorate the Australian and New Zealand landings at Gallipoli in 1915. Australian and British troops form the catafalque party, while their U.S. counterparts raise the flags of the three coalition countries. *(Commonwealth of Australia photo by Darren Hilder. Copyright © Commonwealth of Australia)*

◄

Soldiers from Company B, 3d Battalion, 15th Infantry Regiment, secure the perimeter of a search area. The clock tower in the background was part of an amusement park in the western part of Baghdad.
(Dennis Steele, ARMY Magazine)

▲
Maj. Mark Thompson, the chaplain of 2d Brigade, 101st Airborne Division (Air Assault), and interpreter Ayman Hussain pass out school supplies and chat with children at a school in Mosul, Iraq, May 3, 2003. *(U.S. Army photo by Sgt. Michael Bracken)*

▲
Artillery crewmen of Battery B, 2d Battalion, 319th Airborne Field Artillery Regiment, prepare their 105 mm howitzer for action. The artillerymen practice emplacing their weapon within six minutes or less. *(U.S. Army photo by Spc. Jason B. Baker)*

◄
Pfc. Cody Ruiz, a gunner in the Scout Platoon, 3d Battalion, 15th Infantry Regiment.

(Dennis Steele, ARMY Magazine)

A U.S. military convoy rolls past Leading Aircraftsman Darren Hoare, from the Royal Australian Air Force Airfield Defence Guard detachment, as he patrols the roads around the Australian section of Baghdad International Airport. *(Commonwealth of Australia photo by Darren Hilder. Copyright © Commonwealth of Australia)*

▲

United Kingdom Warrant Officer Mark Stannard,
1 Duke of Wellington's Regiment, delivers a pres-
entation to nearly 50 school girls on the dangers
of unexploded ordnance (UXO) May 15, 2003, in
Az Zubayr. Along with being warned to avoid
UXO, children were taught to seek help from a
soldier should they encounter it.

(U.S. Army photo by Spc. Christopher Selmek)

▲

Ambassador L. Paul Bremer III, head of the
Office of Reconstruction and Humanitarian
Affairs, addresses the media in Mosul on
May 18, 2003, during his familiarization tour
of northern Iraq. Also pictured are: Ghanim Al
Basso, far left, mayor of Mosul and Nineveh
Province, and U.S. Army Maj. Gen. David H.
Petraeus, immediate left, commander, 101st
Airborne Division (Air Assault). *(U.S. Army photo
by Spc. Robert Woodward)*

The 63d Armored Regiment of the 1st Infantry
Division (Mechanized) provides security with
support from an M1A1 Abrams tank and an
M2A3 Bradley Fighting Vehicle in Kirkuk, Iraq,
April 18, 2003. *(U.S. Army photo by Pfc. Brandon Aird)*

▲

Gen. Tommy R. Franks, left, talks with military
police Sgt. Ed Cleland during a visit to Baghdad,
May 27, 2003. *(U.S. Army photo by Sgt. Gustavo Bahena)*

▲
Debra Dever greets her son, Spc. Roger Dever, 1st Battalion, 39th Field Artillery, 3d Infantry Division (Mechanized), at a homecoming ceremony at Fort Stewart, Ga., on June 3, 2003. More than 400 soldiers of the artillery and the Division Band were the first units of the division to return home since the onset of Operation Iraqi Freedom. *(U.S. Army photo by Sgt. Sam Hoffman)*

▲
Seen through a night-vision device, 1st Armored Division soldiers maintain security while searching buildings in Baghdad for weapons, ammo and other illegal items in June 2003. *(U.S. Army photo by Sgt. Jeremiah Lancaster)*

▲
President George W. Bush thanks troops of the coalition forces for their service in Operation Iraqi Freedom during a visit to Doha, Qatar, on June 5, 2003. *(DoD photo)*

On June 5, 2003, President George W. Bush visited the forward headquarters of U.S. Central Command at Doha, Qatar. He spoke to American, Australian, British and Polish service members at the base.

President Bush remembered those who died in the operation to liberate Iraq: "We fight for freedom, and we sacrifice for freedom, and we have lost some of our finest." He said those who lost their lives served more than just the United States; they served the cause of freedom. "Because of you, America and our friends and allies, those of us who love freedom, are now more secure," the president said. "You have justified the confidence that your country has placed in you. You've served your country well. Your commander in chief is grateful. And as importantly, more importantly, millions of American citizens are grateful for what you have done. You believe in America, and America believes in you."

Reflections
by Dennis Steele

Fighting was heavy when the soldiers of the 3d Battalion, 15th Infantry Regiment, with me in tow, one of the unit's embedded journalists, hit Baghdad on April 7, 2003. The soldiers had loaded their vehicles with extra ammunition, and I had stuffed the pockets of my body armor with digital camera data cards and batteries to photograph as much of the expected fight as possible. The initial firefight lasted more than seven hours, and we all conserved our respective kinds of ammunition. No one knew if the fight would continue for days or even weeks. Everyone believed that the battle to take Baghdad would be long fought. But it wasn't.

The defense of Baghdad was either half hearted or half baked—take your pick—and most organized resistance collapsed within 48 hours. When the realization hit us that the battle was over, I inventoried my data cards and began to feel dejected because many were empty. I felt badly about all the photographs that I could have taken if only I had known that I didn't need to nurse my digital storage capacity. The main thing was that I didn't want to let my buddies down—the soldiers with whom I'd spent most of two months in the deserts of Kuwait and Iraq.

I've spent much of my professional time as an embedded journalist—especially since Sept. 11, 2001, the day this war began—following soldiers from several units in Afghanistan, Iraq and other places. As in other contexts involving military unit cohesion, the relationship between an embedded photojournalist and the soldiers of "his" unit is intensely personal. It is a rare privilege to be invited into the circle of a group of American soldiers, especially in combat. I thank every soldier with whom I have served for that privilege. Above everything else, I have never wanted to let soldiers down by doing a poor job. I sincerely hope, in their eyes, that I haven't done that here, and that I never will.

Dennis Steele
ARMY Magazine

Reflections
by Gen. Gordon Sullivan

Almost 50 years of experience with and around America's soldiers causes me to react with pride to our Army's service to the nation in this time of emergency, but not to be surprised that their actions have been exemplary. American soldiers have served with distinction from before our country had a government independent of foreign influence or a government with a Constitution.

Our Army has been a barometer of the American spirit. The fortunes and attitudes of America's soldiers have followed our country's experience, and its strengths and weaknesses over time have been forged in the universal kiln of the national experience.

When Americans look at our soldiers, they see America as they want it to be—selfless, dedicated, competent, cheerful, compassionate, hanging tough for the long haul, whatever it may be. They see men and women of all colors, creeds, sizes and shapes, dedicated to preserving our way of life, and confident that their cause is right and that their mission will be accomplished.

During Operation Iraqi Freedom, it has been said, a news reporter finished his broadcast asking, "Where do we get such men and women?" The answer is simple. We get them from America.

Gordon R. Sullivan
General, United States Army, Retired
32d Chief of Staff of the United States Army

Logistics, Innovation and the 21st Century Soldier

Appendix

This appendix presents glimpses of the magnitude of logistical support, technological innovation and individual equipment for the soldiers of today.

Logistics

Prepositioning. As of mid-2003, the United States Army had more than 200,000 soldiers deployed into the U.S. Central Command's area of responsibility. The majority of the forces served Operation Enduring Freedom and Operation Iraqi Freedom. The Army was responsible for equipping and supporting not only its own soldiers, but those of the other service branches and coalition partners as well.

The United States Army Materiel Command summarized highlights of these supporting endeavors in a briefing titled, "Equipping the Warfighter: Operation Iraqi Freedom," in May 2003. The command noted that the campaign in Iraq was the first war fought using prepositioned equipment. The prepositioning strategy consisted of having supplies, equipment and vehicles in place in Kuwait before the arrival of the combat units. This reduced the stress upon strategic airlift and sealift resources, and enabled units to reach combat readiness more quickly.

Prior to the start of combat, two ships carrying 6,432,000 Meals, Ready-to-Eat (MRE) were dispatched to the Persian Gulf. Two other ships transported 58,000 tons of ammunition of all types. An additional 8,000 tons of ammunition and more than 17,000 vehicles were positioned ahead of the war on the ground in Qatar and Kuwait.

◄

Paratroopers of the 504th Parachute Infantry Regiment in "full battle rattle" gear in Afghanistan, March 2003. *(U.S. Army photo by Staff Sgt. Leopold Medina Jr.)*

The U.S. Army Materiel Command

Innovation

The United States Army owed its successes in Operation Enduring Freedom and Operation Iraqi Freedom to the high levels of training, discipline and courage of its soldiers. New technological innovations aided the soldiers in achieving the multitude of missions assigned.

Meeting Demand

Once the battle started on March 20, 2003, the requirements for continuous support expanded. The 307,000 troops now in the combat zone required an average of 2.1 million gallons of potable water each day. To feed the troops during the three weeks of the intensive ground campaign, Army Materiel Command calculated that it delivered enough MREs to feed the city of Spokane, Wash., for one year. (The 2000 census counted 195,629 persons in Spokane.)

The wheeled and armored vehicles in the units that advanced into Iraq consumed 15 million gallons of fuel every day. According to Army Materiel Command calculations, that is about the same amount of fuel as consumed in the entire state of Florida in one day.

Much of the Army's communications equipment must be portable, and relies on batteries for operating power. One of the more common batteries is called the BA 5590. The demand for batteries expanded sharply in the buildup and combat in Iraq. Production grew to 300,000 batteries per month, reaching the limits of the industrial base.

Information technologies made it possible for leaders and soldiers at all levels and locations to share an accurate awareness of the situation. Blue Force Tracking (BFT) is among the innovations mentioned frequently as having a profound positive influence on mission achievement. BFT evolved from the Army's long-running digitization programs and the advances in communications and computer technology, married with the Global Positioning System. The BFT system was developed by the Army's Program Executive Office for Command, Control & Communications Tactical. The MITRE Corp. was the system engineer/architect. Bruce Robinson of MITRE summarizes the BFT capabilities as answering three essential questions for the user: "Where am I?, where are my buddies?, and where is the enemy?"

Central Baghdad appears in the display of a **Blue Force Tracking (BFT) system** installed in a Humvee. The BFT system allows soldiers to keep track of their locations and communicate with each other via radio and e-mail. *(U.S. Army photo by Daniel Harabin, Tobyhanna Army Depot)*

The system performed flawlessly in Operation Iraqi Freedom. Commanders throughout the theater of operations and senior leaders at the Pentagon could watch the forces as they moved across the field of battle.

In the units equipped with BFT, soldiers could see their position on maps displayed on the video monitors in their aircraft and in wheeled and tracked vehicles. They could also communicate with each other and their commanders through radio and e-mail.

The system also proved invaluable in logistics operations. Logisticians could find out the location of essential supplies and direct them precisely to the units needing the resupply.

Gerry Musto, a mechanical engineering technician in Tobyhanna Army Depot's Production Engineering Directorate, checks the setting on a Blue Force Tracking (BFT) system mounted in a Humvee. Tobyhanna is installing hundreds of BFT systems in vehicles and shelters worldwide. *(U.S. Army photo by Daniel Harabin, Tobyhanna Army Depot)*

The 21st Century Soldier

Feeding the Troops

The Meal, Ready-to-Eat, Individual, or MRE, is the standard military field ration for all the armed services. The MRE replaced the C-Ration in the 1980s and has been continuously updated in succeeding decades. According to the developers at the Soldier Systems Center (Natick), soldier preferences and nutritional values play vital roles in the evolution of the rations.

Twenty-four MRE menus exist in mid-2003. Examples include traditional entrees such as Spaghetti with Meat Sauce and the menu shown in the photo, Beef Steak with Mushroom Gravy. Four vegetarian menus are also among the choices. Menus with an ethnic influence include Beef Teriyaki and Seafood Jambalaya.

MREs maintain their quality in storage for a minimum of three years at 80 degrees Fahrenheit or up to six months at 100 degrees Fahrenheit. Each MRE provides an average of 1,250 kilocalories (13 percent protein, 36 percent fat, 51 percent carbohydrate).

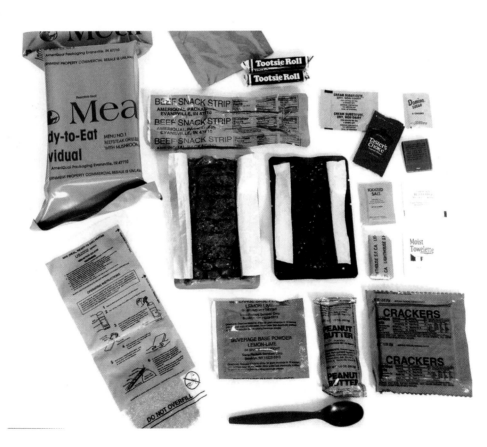

Components of MRE Menu 1 include Beef Steak with Mushroom Gravy plus western style beans, peanut butter, cracker, beef jerky, beverage base with sugar, plastic spoon and flameless ration heater. The accessory pack contains coffee, cream substitute, sugar, salt, chewing gum matches, toilet tissue, towelette, candy and ground red pepper. *(Sarah Underhill, U.S. Army Soldier Systems Center)*

Equipping for Combat

After nearly 227 years, the Army activated its first organization with responsibility for managing the acquisition of everything a soldier wears or carries. The organization is titled Program Executive Office (PEO), Soldier.

PEO, Soldier defines its mission this way: "To arm and equip soldiers to dominate the full spectrum of peace and war, now and in the future." The organization's 346 programs are organized under three project managers. They are: Project Manager, Soldier Warrior; Project Manager, Soldier Weapons; and Project Manager, Soldier Sensors and Equipment.

The information above and the photos on these pages are provided courtesy of PEO, Soldier. The photos present a sampling of individual equipment for soldiers of the United States Army of the early 21st century.

Knee and Elbow Pads (KEPs) provide dismounted soldiers with added protection. The pads are ambidextrous. KEPs are constructed of a molded, high-density polyethylene knee or elbow shell fastened to a Cordura woodland camouflage fabric outer cover that is sewn to a polyester inner lining. Within these coverings is sewn a three-segment impact-cushioning polyethylene foam. The knee pads weigh 9.0 ounces, and the elbow pads weigh 3.6 ounces. *(PEO, Soldier photo)*

Body armor provides protective capability to stop or slow down fragments and reduce the number of wounds. The latest version is called Interceptor Body Armor (IBA). IBA is modular, multiple-threat body armor composed of ergonomically designed front and back plates, and an outer tactical vest. The total system weighs 16.4 pounds. Attachable throat and groin protectors provide increased protection. Webbing attachment loops on the front of the vest allow soldiers to tailor loads to meet mission needs. *(PEO, Soldier photo)*

The one-quart canteen with cover is kidney-shaped. It consists of a body, strap and cap, plus fabric cover (not shown). The cap allows the soldier to drink from the canteen without removing the M40A1 chemical-biological mask. *(PEO, Soldier photo)*

The Desert Combat Boot is made with moisture-resistant leather in the foot portion of the boot, with a textured nylon duck upper. The boot has a rubber "Panama" design and an abrasion-resistant outsole. The insole is a leather foam combination that provides insulation from the ground. It features a lace-and-closed-loop speed lace system.

(PEO, Soldier photo)

The Helmet, Ground Troops and Parachutists, is a rigid one-piece ballistic protective item made of Aramid fabric with a phenolic/PVB resin. It has a small visor and contains a cradle suspension system. The headband utilizes hook-and-loop tape to adjust for head circumference and to attach the headband to the suspension assembly. The chin strap is a two-point, open chin cup design. A camouflage cover comes in several patterns.

(PEO, Soldier photo)

The Combat Vehicle Crewman Helmet consists of a rigid, compression molded, outer shell constructed with 33 layers of Aramid Kevlar fabric. The shell has a rubber edging adhesive along its peripheral contour, and is painted with a chemical agent-resistive coating. The liner is constructed with energy absorbing foam sections enclosed in a fire-resistant Nomex mesh fabric. *(PEO, Soldier photo)*

The **Advanced Combat Helmet** with the AN/PVS-14 Night Vision Device comes in two shell sizes and two pad sizes. The helmet shell is Aramid fabric in Camouflage Green 383. The AN/PVS-14 monocular night-vision device is a lightweight, multipurpose apparatus. The system features a projected infrared light-emitting diode for short-range illumination for such activities as map reading. The AN/PVS-14 is supplied with the military head strap for hands-free use.

(PEO, Soldier photo)

The **Field Case** holds a first aid kit or compass. It attaches to the equipment belt or suspenders with a slide keeper.

(PEO, Soldier photo)

Acknowledgments

The staff members at the Association of the United States Army deserve thanks for their assistance in conceiving this book and bringing it into being. Thanks also are due to the staff at the Naval Institute Press for their contributions to its development and publication.

A team of dedicated and talented professionals created and produced the book. Simone Hammarstrand coordinated photo acquisitions. Nina D. Seebeck edited and proofread the text and captions. Amy B. Thompson created the index. Liz Weaver of Hinge Incorporated designed the book, assisted by Aaron Weinstein.

Dozens of persons assisted the Association of the United States Army and the production team in finding appropriate photographs. We are grateful to every one of them for their willing assistance. The persons listed below merit special thanks.

Australian Ministry of Defence: *Rod Dudfield*

Combined Forces Land Component Command: *Sgt. 1st Class David K. Dismukes, Gary Jones*

Department of Defense Joint Combat Camera Center: *Staff Sgt. Gina O'Bryan, USAF*

Department of Transportation, Maritime Administration: *Bill Kurfehs, Steve Jackson*

V Corps: *Maj. William D. Thurmond*

4th Infantry Division (Mechanized): *Debra Bingham*

General Dynamics Land Systems: *Liz Buscemie, Peter M. Keating*

MITRE Corp.: *Lisa Muro, Bruce Robinson, Alan Shoemaker*

MPRI, an L-3 Company: *Rick Kiernan*

National Guard Bureau: *Col. Mark Allen*

Office of Chief of Public Affairs, Department of the Army: *Col. Jim Allen, Maj. Martha Brooks, Col. Joseph G. Curtin, Brig. Gen. Robert Gaylord, Charles A. Krohn, Robert Melhorn*

Office of Chief, U.S. Army Reserve: *Albert Schilf*

Office of the Secretary of the Army: *Maj. Don Bolduc, Lt. Col. John W. Nicholson*

Office of the Surgeon General, U.S. Army: *Lyn Kukral*

Program Executive Office, Soldier: *Debra Dawson*

10th Mountain Division (Light Infantry): *Spc. Steven McGowan*

Tobyhanna Army Depot: *Anthony Ricchiazzi, Kevin M. Toolan*

United Defense: *Paul Anderson, Doug Coffey*

United Kingdom Ministry of Defence: *Ash Amliwala, D. A. Belson*

U.S. Army Community and Family Support Center: *Harriet Rice*

U.S. Army Europe: *Joseph Garvey, Robert Purtiman*

U.S. Army Materiel Command: *Anita Hodges, Brenda Taylor*

U.S. Army Soldier Systems Center: *Janice Rosado, Patricia Welsh*

U.S. Army Space and Missile Defense Command: *Debra Valine*

U.S. Army Space Command: *Michael Howard, Sharon L. Hartman, Maj. Laura D. Kenney*

U.S. Army Special Operations Command: *Sgt. 1st Class Blake R. Waltman*

U.S. Central Command: *Petty Officer Gary Bonaccorso, James Wilkinson*

U.S. Transportation Command: *James Matthews*

Resources

Publications

Doubler, Michael D. *Guarding the Homeland: The Army National Guard and Homeland Security.* Arlington, Va.: Association of the United States Army, December 2002.

Moseley, Lt. Gen. T. Michael, USAF. *Operation Iraqi Freedom—By the Numbers.* Shaw Air Force Base, S.C.: Commander, Combined Forces Air Component Command, April 30, 2003.

Soldier Systems Center (Natick). *Operational Rations of the Department of Defense.* Natick Pamphlet 30–25, 5th Ed. Natick, Mass. April 2002.

Magazines

ARMY Magazine, the monthly professional journal published by the Association of the United States Army. Issues consulted from Nov. 2001 (Vol. 51, No. 11) through June 2003 (Vol. 53, No. 7).

Newspapers

AUSA News, the newspaper published monthly by the Association of the United States Army. Issues consulted from Nov. 2001 (Vol. 25, No. 1) through July 2003 (Vol. 26, No. 9).

Briefings

U.S. Army Materiel Command. "Equipping the Warfighter: Operation Iraqi Freedom. From Fuel Bags…to Batteries…to Bombs." Alexandria, Va.: U.S. Army Materiel Command, May 2003.

Recurring reports

Department of Defense. "National Guard and Reserve Units Called to Active Duty." Washington, D.C.: A complete unit listing organized by service, state and communities within each state. Updated weekly.

Web sites

Web sites provide rapid access to great stores of information. However, addresses and locations change frequently. Therefore, the listing below is limited to addresses that are less likely to change. Each of the addresses contains links, search capabilities and archives. Readers interested in acquiring more information will be rewarded by visiting the sites and exploring each one.

Association of the United States Army: http://www.ausa.org

United States Army Home Page: http://www.army.mil
   A treasure trove of Army information is found here. It is well-organized and easy to use.

U.S. Army National Guard: http://www.arng.army.mil/soldier_resources

U.S. Army Reserve: http://www.army.mil/usar

Department of Defense: http://www.defenselink.mil

U.S. Central Command: http://www.centcom.mil

U.S. Army Forces, Central Command (and Combined Forces Land Component Command): http://www.arcent.army.mil

Family Topics

Army Family Liaison Office: http://www.aflo.org

Community and Family Support Center: http://www.cfsc.army.mil

National Military Family Association: http://www.nmfa.org

Army Community Service: http://www.goacs.org

Index

Italics indicate photographs or illustrations.

An alert Chinook helicopter crew chief in flight over Afghanistan, 2002. *(Dennis Steele, ARMY Magazine)*

Index to Photographers